THE QUILT-BLOCK HISTORY OF PIONEER DAYS

WITH PROJECTS KIDS CAN MAKE

BY MARY COBB

Illustrated
by Jan Davey Ellis

The Millbrook Press
Brookfield, Connecticut

Library of Congress Cataloging-in Publication Data
Cobb, Mary.
The quilt-block history of pioneer days: with projects kids
can make/by Mary Cobb; illustrated by Jan Davey Ellis.
p.   cm.
Includes bibliographical references and index.
Summary: This brightly illustrated book shows
how traditional American quilt-block designs
tell the story of pioneer days, when designs
were created to reflect daily life and special
events. Simple craft projects, using paper and
other easily obtained materials, are included.
ISBN 1-56294-485-1 (lib. bdg.)
1. Quilting—United States—History—Juvenile literature.
2. Handicraft—Juvenile literature.   3. Frontier and pioneer life—
United States—Juvenile literature.   [1. Quilts.   2. Frontier and
pioneer life.   3. Handicraft.]   I. Ellis, Jan Davey, ill.
II. Title.
TT835.C62   1995   746.9′7′0973—dc20   94-9279   CIP   AC

Published by The Millbrook Press
2 Old New Milford Road
Brookfield, Connecticut 06804

CONTENTS

THE QUILT-BLOCK HISTORY OF PIONEER DAYS

QUILTS AND HISTORY

A quilt is a warm bedcovering made of three layers—top, padding, and backing—that are stitched or tied together with thread. Perhaps you have a warm, comfortable quilt on your bed. But did you know that the patchwork designs of many quilts tell the story of pioneer days?

In the 1600s, many people who lived in Europe left their homes and sailed to America to start a new life. They lived together in small settlements called colonies. The colonies were ruled by countries in Europe. By 1700, Great Britain controlled a string of colonies along the eastern coast of what is today the United States.

The people in the colonies, or colonists, needed food, shelter, and clothing. There were no stores or supplies in the wilderness, so the colonists had to bring with them everything they would need to begin life in their new land. Among the things the colonists brought were many quilts. It would be a long time before new quilts could be made.

In early America, fabric was scarce and costly. And before new fabric could be made, sheep would have to be raised for wool, or flax grown and harvested for linen. Wool and linen fibers would have to be spun into thread, and the thread woven into cloth.

In the meantime, the old quilts began to wear out. The women patched and patched the quilts with small pieces of fabric left over from making clothing or cut from old, worn-out clothes. Before long, the old quilts took on a whole new look. The patches on the quilts seemed to form designs.

Of course, even with the most careful mending, the old quilts finally wore out. New ones had to be made. Scraps of cloth were carefully saved for quilt making. The women cut the pieces of fabric into squares, triangles, and rectangles. They remembered the old patched quilts, and they sewed the new shapes together to form designs called quilt blocks.

The quilt blocks were then joined together to make a quilt top. These early quilts often had fleece from sheep, old rags, raw cotton, or even dried leaves for padding. The quilt backing was usually made from several large pieces of fabric. Then the three layers were sewn or tied together to form the quilt.

For many years there was plenty of land along the eastern coast of North America for anyone who wanted to build a home, raise a family, and grow crops for themselves and their livestock. But more and more colonists came from Europe. These people also wanted land for their homes and farms. At the same time, the children of earlier colonists grew up, married, and had families of their own. They wanted good land to farm, too.

SIMPLE QUILT BLOCKS

The simplest quilt blocks were usually the most popular patterns for every-day quilts. The women did not have much spare time, so they chose basic designs and patterns. Here are four blocks often used in a girl's first quilt.

SIMPLE FOUR-PATCH

TRIP AROUND THE WORLD

AUTUMN TINTS

PATIENCE NINE-PATCH

In 1783, after a long struggle, the people in Britain's North American colonies won their independence and founded the United States. But by this time, the land along the eastern coast was crowded with cities and villages. Good land for homes and farms was becoming scarce and expensive. Where could new families live?

To the west, land was inexpensive and sometimes even free for the asking. Much of this land was flat and good for farming. In 1785, the Congress of the United States began selling land between the Appalachian Mountains and the Mississippi River for $1 an acre to people who were willing to explore and settle the land.

Many families who lived in the East decided to move west. They became known as pioneers or settlers. By the early 1800s, pioneer families had crossed the Mississippi River and the Great Plains, then called the Great American Desert. By the 1840s they had climbed the Rocky Mountains and reached Oregon and California. Eventually all these areas became part of the United States. In this way the country grew from the Atlantic Ocean to the Pacific Ocean.

As the settlers moved west, they cleared land, built homes, and founded many small towns, some of which are today big cities. They took many quilts with them because winters were often cold and stormy. Quilts were also used to keep the family's valuables from breaking during the bumpy wagon ride west. And the quilts served as cushions and beds for the weary travelers.

The pioneer families were proud of their quilts. Quilt blocks were created and named for special events in their lives. Quilt blocks were made to honor important events and people in American history. But many quilt blocks were named for everyday parts of pioneer life. They were a way for pioneer women to tell the story of the settling of the country in a very special art form.

A SIMPLE NINE-PATCH COLLAGE

A simple quilt block can be made from nine squares. Children were taught to make nine-patch quilt blocks as soon as they could handle a needle.

To make this collage you will need magazines, scissors, paste, the square template, and a copy of the nine-patch quilt block.

Use the template to cut squares of color from magazine pages. Paste them over the quilt block. Now you have a nine-patch quilt block.

SQUARE TEMPLATE

SIMPLE NINE-PATCH QUILT BLOCK

SAYING GOOD-BYE

It was not easy to pack up and move west. Traveling was very difficult. And it was a sad time for many families, especially for the relatives and friends who would be staying behind in the East. Still, the families went west seeking a better way of life.

Before a family began a westward journey, often friends, neighbors, and relatives would hold a grand good-bye party for the travelers. The women would meet secretly and plan an album quilt.

An album quilt was a very special quilt made for a family or friend who was moving west. The quilt makers would agree upon a certain album block, and then each person in the group would make up the quilt block in their own choice of fabrics. Each block was signed by the maker. The blocks were then assembled, quilted, and presented at the going-away party.

The album quilt was a way for a family to remember their friends and relatives. It was packed inside the covered wagon in a special safe place. When the pioneer family had built a new home in the wilderness, the album quilt was displayed in a place of honor. It was a colorful reminder of those loved ones who had stayed behind.

ALBUM QUILT BLOCKS

Quilt makers used many different quilt-block designs to make album quilts. Here are four popular quilt blocks used in album quilts.

ALBUM

AUTOGRAPH

HOLE IN THE BARN DOOR

SIGNATURE

QUILT BLOCK BOOKMARKS

A bookmark is a nice gift to make for a friend. You will need scissors, markers or crayons, and construction paper. Reproduce the bookmarks on the paper. Color the quilt block. Sign your name inside the block design. Put your friend's name on the lines.

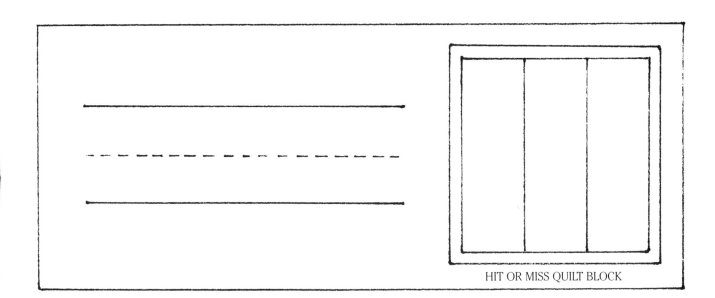

HIT OR MISS QUILT BLOCK

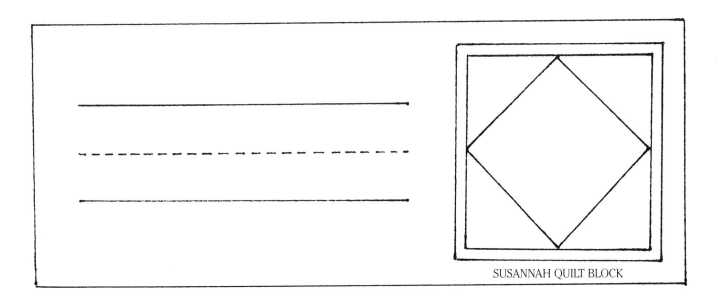

SUSANNAH QUILT BLOCK

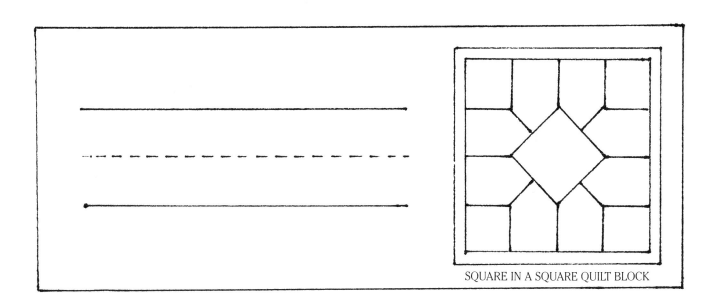

SQUARE IN A SQUARE QUILT BLOCK

3
GOING WEST

What was it like to move west? Just as moving to a new home is exciting and hard work today, so it was two hundred years ago. First, the pioneer families would have a yard sale. The house, furniture, land, and livestock would be sold.

The money from the sale would be used to buy a wagon, a team of oxen to pull the wagon, and all the things that the family would need for the long trip west, as well as supplies for a year in the wilderness.

Food, clothing, pots and pans, bedding, medicine, seeds, tools, guns, and ammunition were carefully packed inside the wagon. Quilts were laid over the barrels and packing boxes to make temporary beds for the family.

Getting to the frontier was a difficult task. Early roads west followed trails made by animals and Indians. The earliest wagon route west to the Ohio River region was Gist's Trace, built in 1753. It ran from Maryland to what is today Pittsburgh, Pennsylvania.

In 1775, Daniel Boone blazed a trail across the Appalachian Mountains through the Cumberland Gap. This trail became the Wilderness Road, probably the most important road for the pioneers moving from the eastern seaboard across the mountains.

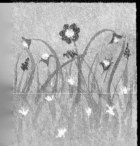

PIONEER TRAILS

Fort Vancouver

OREGON TRAIL

CALIFORNIA TRAIL

MORMON TRAIL

MORMON TRAIL

OREGON TRAIL

Salt Lake City

Sacramento

SANTA FE TRAIL

Santa Fe

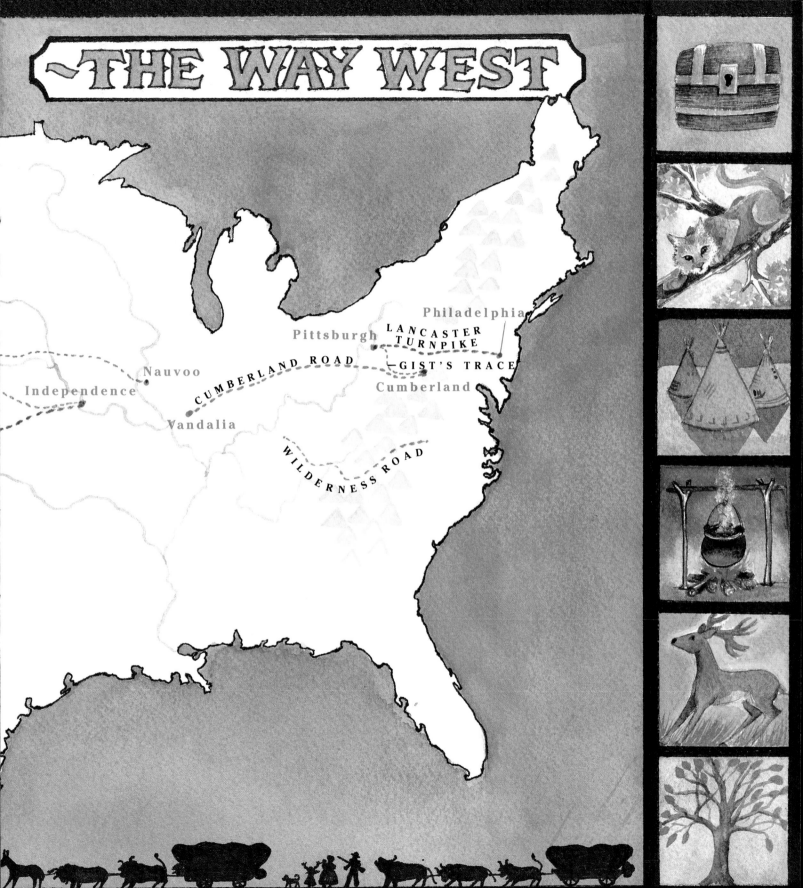

~THE WAY WEST

Philadelphia

Pittsburgh LANCASTER
TURNPIKE

CUMBERLAND ROAD ~GIST'S TRACE

Nauvoo Cumberland

Independence

Vandalia

WILDERNESS ROAD

Many pioneers crossed Pennsylvania on the Lancaster Turnpike, which led to the Ohio River. Here the families could load their possessions on river boats and travel the Ohio River westward all the way to the Mississippi River. From the Mississippi they could continue west along the Missouri River.

At Independence, Missouri, the pioneer families might join a wagon train moving to the Far West along the Oregon Trail, the California Trail, or the Santa Fe Trail, or one of the branches of those trails, such as the Mormon Trail. These western trails were used from the 1820s to the 1860s, when trains began to cross the country.

Each year, pioneers would start rolling west in early April to get to the new lands before snow fell. Days on the trail began before 4:00 A.M. The travelers had to fix their breakfast, milk the cows, and reload the wagons before starting out. On the trail mothers and children walked behind the wagon while fathers drove the team. Mothers carried little babies and held the hands of the toddlers. Only those who were very sick or injured were allowed to ride inside the wagon.

The wagons moved slowly. Following the wagons were cows, extra horses, oxen, and sheep. It was the job of the older children to drive the livestock and watch that the animals did not stray into the wilderness. Even having to guide stubborn animals, walking was far and away easier than bumping along in the wagon over the rutty trails.

Because there were no bridges, streams and rivers had to be forded. Hills and mountains had to be climbed, and often, just as the family had arrived safely at the bottom of a mountain, another mountain loomed in their path.

Good days were great for traveling. On stormy days the rain put out cooking fires, scattered the livestock, and soaked everything and everybody. After a rainstorm, clothing and quilts were hung on the wagon to dry.

It might surprise you to know that the grown-up pioneers often wished they had not left the comfort of their homes in the East to make the journey. Mothers and fathers worried that their children would be lost forever in the wilderness, eaten by wild animals, or taken by Indians. For these reasons children had to stay close to the wagons.

Parents were often tired, cross, and hungry. Children were often tired, cross, and hungry, too—but for all that, most of the young people found pleasure in each new day. For the rest of their lives, they remembered the wagon ride west.

THE WAY WEST QUILT BLOCKS

Getting to the West was probably the hardest part of relocating in a new land. The pioneers never forgot the journey west. Quilt blocks told the story of rocky trails, hills, and valleys along the route of the covered wagons.

ROCKY ROAD TO KANSAS

TRAIL OF THE COVERED WAGONS

HILL AND VALLEY

ROCKY GLEN

BROKEN DISHES PUZZLE

Even with careful packing, dishes were often broken on the bumpy wagon ride to the West. This was sad because dishes were hard to replace on the frontier. The sharp points of the broken dishes quilt block reminded the pioneers of the jagged pieces of their broken dishes.

To make a broken dishes puzzle you will need three colors of construction paper, scissors, the triangle template shown here, and an envelope. Copy the template and use it as a pattern to cut two triangles from each of two colors of paper. Cut four triangles from the remaining color. Use the triangles to form a quilt block. When you are finished, store your puzzle pieces in an envelope.

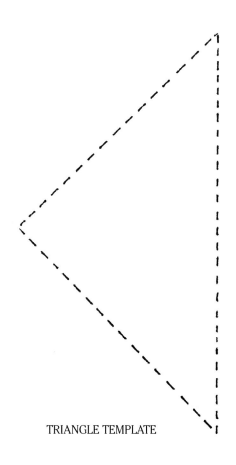

TRIANGLE TEMPLATE

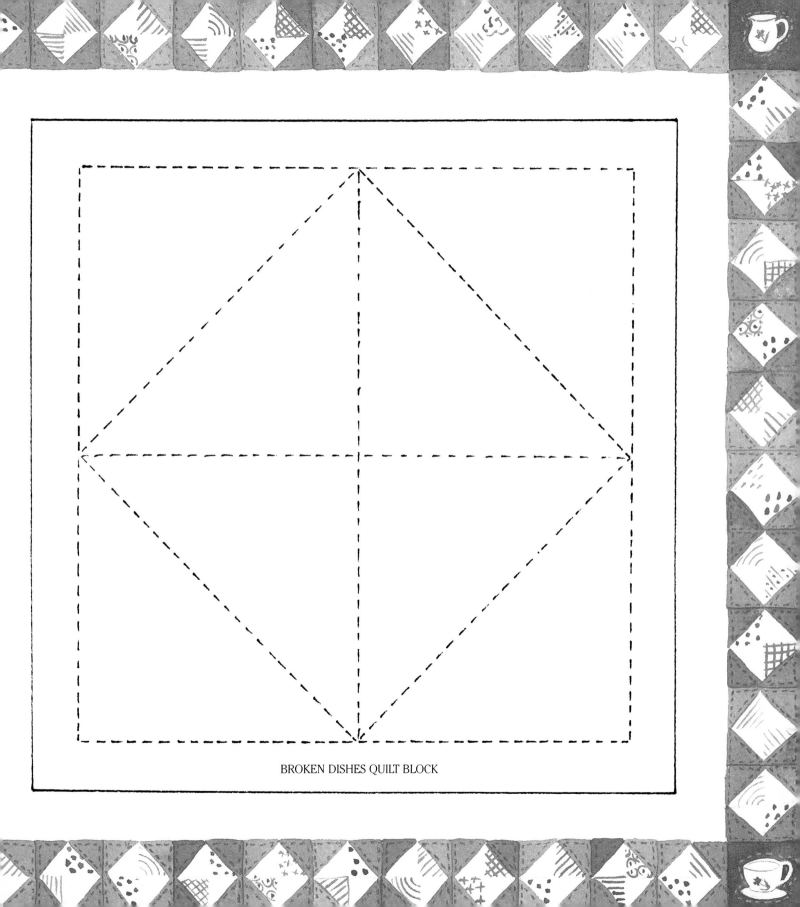

BROKEN DISHES QUILT BLOCK

BUILDING THE CABIN

However hard the trip west, the pioneers rejoiced when they reached their new land. For a time, the families lived in their wagons or in tents or crude lean-tos. The first winter was usually spent clearing the homesite and building a log cabin. On the Plains, there were few trees. Families built homes from blocks of sod—the thickly rooted grass that covered the land for miles in all directions.

Where trees were plentiful, the tallest and straightest were chosen for the cabin. The trees were chopped down and hauled to the clearing. The logs were notched at each end and then lifted one atop the other to build the cabin's walls.

While a father worked to finish the cabin, the mother and children filled the spaces between the logs to make the house draft-proof. If the spaces were large, sticks were forced into the gaps, and then the cracks were packed with mud or clay.

Once the walls were up, the roof was framed and shingled. A fireplace and chimney were built of stones and clay. A window was cut in one wall. Now the cabin was a home, a shelter with a fire giving warmth, light, and comfort to the family.

BUILDING THE CABIN QUILT BLOCKS

How happy the pioneers must have been when they had finally cleared the land and built a cabin. Quilt blocks commemorate these happy events. Fences were important, for they protected the livestock. Waterwheels were used to turn millstones that ground grain into flour or cornmeal. When the pioneers had built their cabins, then it was time to build a little red schoolhouse on a hill.

RAIL FENCE

LOG CABIN

WATERWHEEL

LITTLE RED SCHOOLHOUSE

Sometimes cabins were raised in a day by a house-raising party. On that special day, neighbors came from miles around. Men brought their tools and women brought baskets of food. All day the walls of the house rose higher and higher. After the roof was on the house, a party and dance were held. This was wonderful fun for the pioneer families and a chance for everyone to meet new neighbors and make new friends.

HOUSE-ON-A-HILL
AND
PINE-TREE BORDER

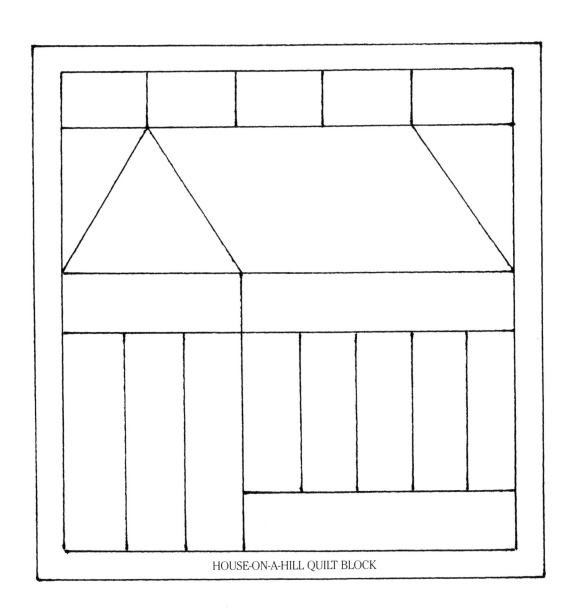

HOUSE-ON-A-HILL QUILT BLOCK

To make a border for your classroom or a bulletin board, you will need scissors, crayons or markers, and copies of the house-on-a-hill quilt block and pine-tree quilt block. Color the blocks, cut them out, and tape them together as a border for the room or mount them on a bulletin board.

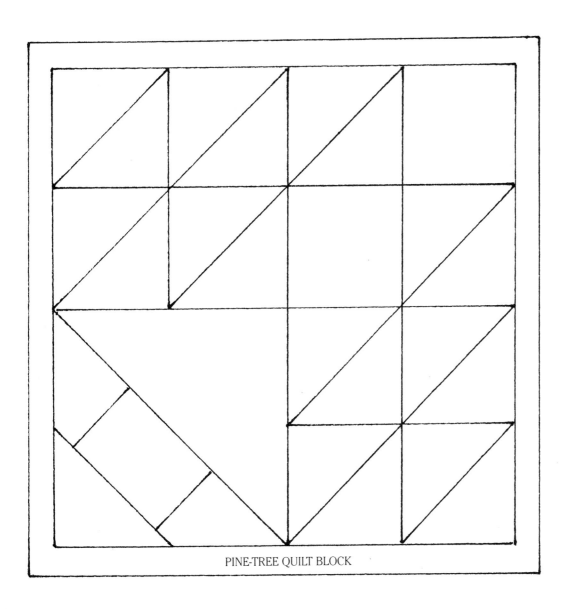

PINE-TREE QUILT BLOCK

When the log cabin was finished, the pioneer family moved into their new home. They had very few furnishings. An upturned log might serve as a chair. Beds were wooden platforms built against the wall. Wooden planks were placed over barrels to serve as a table. Children often slept on a pallet, a small straw mattress, laid by the fireplace.

Babies might sleep in cradles made from packing boxes. Whatever bed you slept in, it would be lumpy and hard, for mattresses were stuffed with dry leaves, corn husks, or straw. Quilts were placed over the mattresses to make sleeping more comfortable.

Clothing was hung on wooden pegs driven into the log walls. Other pegs were positioned over the fireplace or front door to hold the family's long rifle, so that it would be handy in case of an emergency.

The fireplace was the heart of the home. It was used for heat and light as well as for cooking. If the fire went out, a child might have to walk several miles to the nearest neighbor to borrow a kettle of glowing coals to restart the fire.

At night, lighted by flames from the fireplace, candles, or a simple oil lamp, the cabin was a safe haven for the pioneer family.

INSIDE THE CABIN QUILT BLOCKS

Once the cabin was finished the settlers furnished it with pride. Quilt blocks were named for very ordinary furniture and everyday objects in homes. The spool quilt block was named for a thread spool, a shape also found in the posts of a spool bed. Many trips to the woodpile were needed to fill the kitchen woodbox. And how exciting it would be to keep your few possessions in a secret drawer.

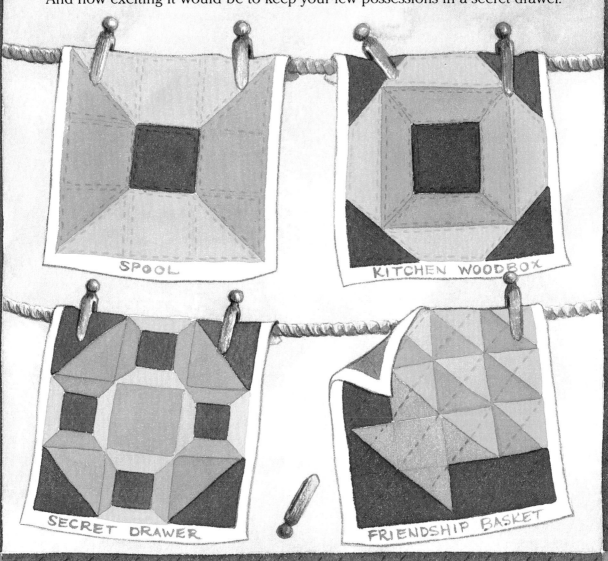

SPOOL

KITCHEN WOODBOX

SECRET DRAWER

FRIENDSHIP BASKET

A SHOOFLY BOX

A shoofly was a rocking chair built for a small child. The shoofly quilt block is one of the best known of all quilt blocks. To make a shoofly box you will need crayons or markers, scissors, glue, and a medium to heavyweight paper. Reproduce the box on paper, color, cut out, fold on dotted lines, and glue tabs in place. Do you have a friend who needs cheering up? Put a treasure in the box and present it to your friend.

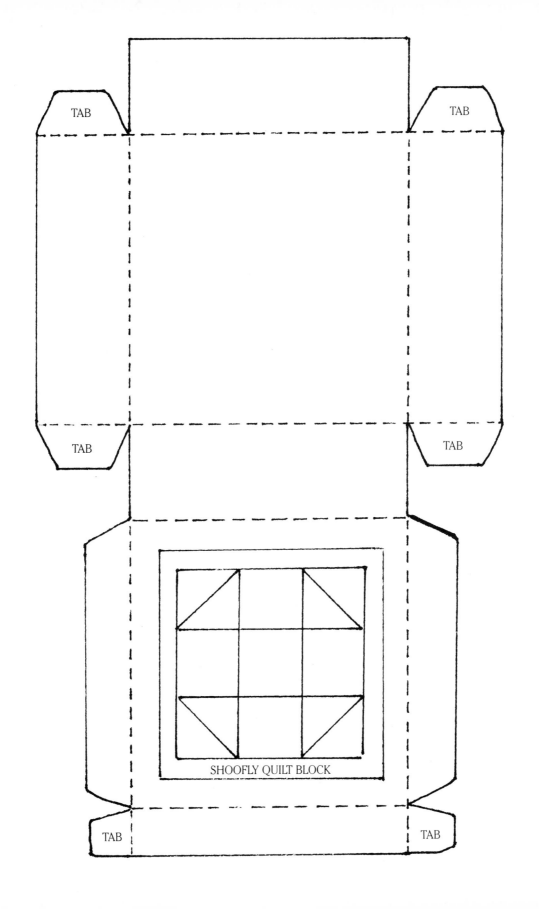

TAB

TAB

TAB

TAB

TAB

TAB

SHOOFLY QUILT BLOCK

6 WORK TO DO

In pioneer days there was work for everyone. Little children learned to help by the time they were two years of age. Young children were expected to feed the chickens, gather eggs, weed the garden, and pick wild nuts and berries. Older children had to help with the heavier work of planting, plowing, tending livestock, haying, hunting and fishing, cooking, washing, and cleaning.

If there were no girls in a pioneer family, the boys had to help with the work inside the cabin as well as outside. If there were no boys, the girls were expected to work in the woods and fields as well as do inside chores.

Two chores kept all the children busy every day of every year. Those were getting firewood and carrying water. The fireplace used stacks and stacks of split wood to keep the cabin warm as well as provide a cooking fire. Water for the animals, and for drinking, cooking, bathing, and laundry had to be carried from a brook or stream. It was a never-ending job.

Mothers worked very hard, too. They tended the babies and took care of sick and injured people. They prepared the food, made and mended clothing for the whole family, raised huge vegetable gardens, sewed quilts,

WORK TO DO QUILT BLOCKS

A pioneer's life in the West held many risks. Every family member had to keep a sharp watch for danger. Unfriendly Indians might come by. But more dangerous were the wild animals that often killed livestock as well as people.

INDIAN HATCHET

CROSSED CANOES

FOX AND GEESE

HOVERING HAWKS

and made soap and candles. When day was done, mothers listened to their children's lessons and heard their prayers.

Fathers had much to do. Where many trees grew, they had to be good axmen. Trees had to be chopped down to clear the land for pastures, fields, and gardens. Fathers raised the livestock and plowed and planted the fields for grain. A pioneer father hunted game for food. He butchered the

animals and cut up the meat and saved the skins to make into leather for jackets, shoes, and harnesses for the oxen and horses.

But far and away the most important job the father had was to protect his family. The pioneers had followed wild game and Indian trails as they went west, and the pioneer father kept a careful watch for Indians and animals that might do his family harm.

BEAR'S PAW GREETING CARD

To make this card you will need scissors, crayons or markers, and medium-weight paper. Copy the card. Cut out the copy, fold on the dotted line, and color the design.

Write a message inside the card for someone who would not be afraid of a bear's paw. How about your dad or grandpa? Grrr!

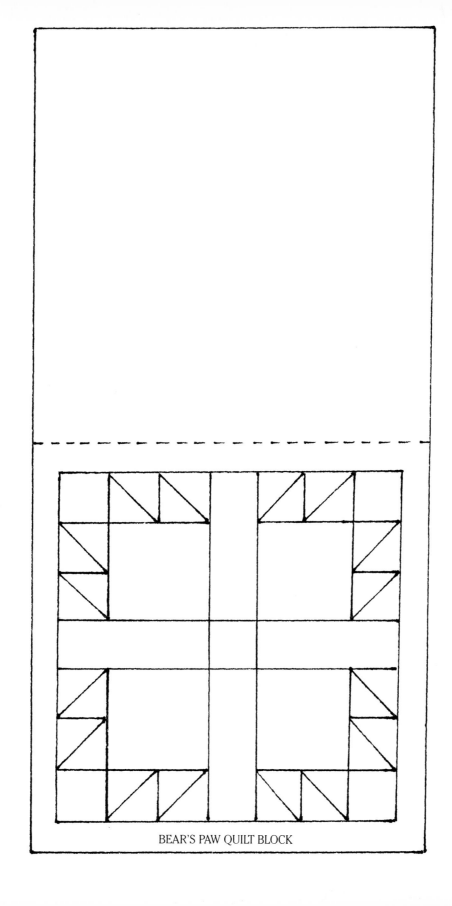

BEAR'S PAW QUILT BLOCK

FOOD AND CLOTHING

Getting enough food and clothing was a serious problem for the pioneer families. The pioneers brought food for the long ride west as well as for the first year in their new home. Much of the food was dried or salted to keep it from spoiling. Even so, food became stale and moldy. Yet eating it was better than going hungry.

As soon as possible, pioneer families cleared land for fields and gardens. The seeds that they had carried with them from the East—corn, squash, pumpkin, parsnip, pea, bean, and turnip—were planted and carefully tended. Some families had even brought apple seeds and saplings, for there were no fruit trees in the wilderness.

The pioneer boys and men hunted game for meat. Where there were rivers and streams, the families fished. Salt was a necessity, to preserve meat and fish for winter, so the settlers watched and followed the wild animals to find a salt lick, a place where a natural deposit of salt lay near the surface of the earth.

Sugar was very scarce. White sugar came from the West Indies in a loaf or cone weighing as much as eight to ten pounds. A cone of sugar cost more

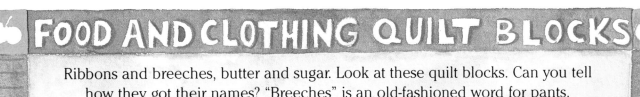

Ribbons and breeches, butter and sugar. Look at these quilt blocks. Can you tell how they got their names? "Breeches" is an old-fashioned word for pants. Ribbons were prized and saved for special dress-up occasions. Sugar came in large cones wrapped in paper. A churn was used to produce golden butter. A paddle called a dasher in the churn stirred cream until it thickened.

RIBBONS

BREECHES

CHURN DASH

SUGAR CONE

than a dollar, the same amount of money that could buy a family a year's worth of flour. Sometimes honey was used as a sweetener. But for the most part, the pioneers went without sweet treats.

In season, the pioneer children picked berries, some of which were dried and saved. In the fall, nuts were gathered and stored.

In the pioneer home all the cooking was done over the open fire on the hearth. Meat and vegetables were cooked together to make a large stew. Indian corn that pioneers grew was eaten at every meal, in many ways. Corn was used in porridge, pudding, and corn bread. Pioneer food was plain and simple, but after a day of hard work it brought smiles to the faces of the tired, hungry family.

Most pioneer families took along extra clothing or cloth for making new clothes. When children outgrew their clothing, it was handed down to the younger members of the family, as long as the clothing held together. Although the clothing was carefully mended and patched, however, eventually it wore out. Then the families would have to find or make materials from which to make new clothes.

Fabric for clothing was very hard to obtain. If the family had brought sheep from the East, then the women would set up spinning wheels and spin the fleece into yarn and thread for woolen cloth. Flax was planted, and the fibers were spun into thread for linen cloth. It would take several years to save enough thread to weave into cloth for clothing.

If no cloth was available, the pioneers had to dress as the Indians did, in the skins of animals. Animal skins were saved and treated to make tough and flexible leather for shoes, jackets, vests, and breeches. In the pioneer's world nothing was ever wasted or thrown away if some use could be found for it.

CORN AND BEANS RECIPE FOLDER

You will need scissors, markers or crayons, paste, and a copy of the recipe folder reproduced on medium-weight paper. Cut out on solid lines, fold on dotted lines, and glue tabs in back.

Use with copies of the recipe cards.

Use copies of the blank cards for recipes of your own.

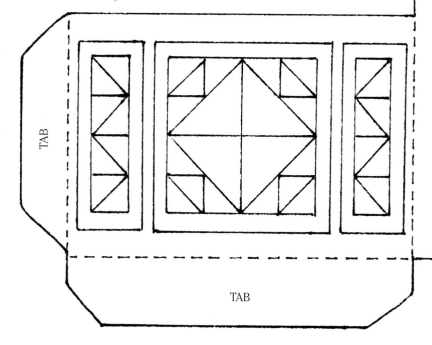

TAB

TAB

CORN-AND-BEANS QUILT BLOCK

CORN BREAD

Prepare a package of corn bread mix according to package directions.

Serve your family the warm corn bread for a pioneer treat.

SUCCOTASH (corn and beans)

1 package of frozen lima beans
1 package frozen corn
½ cup milk
½ stick butter or margarine
salt and pepper

Cook the lima beans and corn according to package directions. Drain the vegetables and return to pot. Add the other ingredients. Heat while stirring. Serve with corn bread.

SPECIAL OCCASIONS

Pioneer families worked long and hard just to have the barest of necessities, but this did not mean that they did not take time for some fun.

Toys were made at home if time allowed. For the most part, children had to make their own toys. Little girls made stick dolls and dressed them in clothes fashioned from scraps of cloth. Boys made slingshots and fishing poles. Both boys and girls liked to explore, hike, race, and swim when their chores were finished.

Women especially looked forward to going to a quilting bee. This was a special day when the women of the neighborhood got together to finish a quilt. On that day an unfinished quilt would be placed on a quilting frame and as many women as could squeeze in sat in chairs around the frame and sewed the quilt together. It was the job of the youngest girls to keep the needles threaded as the women sewed.

While the women worked on the quilt, the men and boys stayed outside or in the barn and helped with farm chores. After a good supper the quilt was taken off the frame and admired by all. Then the chairs and quilt frame were cleared from the room to make room for dancing and merriment.

SPECIAL OCCASIONS QUILT BLOCKS

Pioneer families celebrated the good times in their lives—weddings, births, new neighbors. Many found joy in practicing their faith. Special days were cherished, and quilt blocks were created to honor these red-letter days.

WEDDING RINGS

BABY BLOCKS

NEXT DOOR NEIGHBOR

CROSS AND CROWN

The pioneers got together for husking bees, spelling bees, singing sessions, and weddings. On Sunday, if a traveling preacher was in the neighborhood, everyone who could would go to church. For the children, the church service was a long time to sit and be quiet, but it was a way to see friends and neighbors.

On the whole, the pioneer families found time to enjoy themselves as they worked to make new homes in the West.

DRESDEN PLATE PUNCH WORK

Quilts were held together with rows of tiny stitches called "quilting." You can make this Dresden plate quilt block in punch work, which copies the look of stitching. You will need a copy of the Dresden plate quilt block, a pin, and an old magazine. Place a magazine under the Dresden plate block. Use the pin to make tiny rows of holes along the lines of the design. Work carefully so that you do not prick yourself! When you are finished, hang the block in a window.

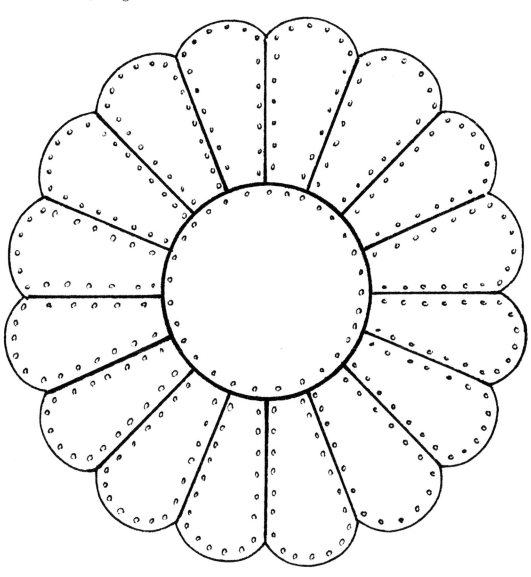

9 THE WEATHER

Day-to-day changes in the weather were of serious concern to the pioneers. On the way west, when the sun shone and the days were warm and dry, the families enjoyed their wilderness life. But when the wind blew and the clouds poured down rain they had to seek shelter in their wagons, tents, or lean-tos. To protect their possessions and themselves, the pioneers learned to keep an eye on the weather.

Pioneers watched the sky as well as the plants and animals to help them forecast changes in the weather. They knew that when the smoke from their campfires hung low over the ground they were in for a storm. And when the swallows and bats swooped low or birds roosted in the trees, rainy weather was on the way.

Red skies at night and geese flying high predicted a spell of good weather. That meant that blue skies and sunny days were ahead.

In their new homes the pioneers endured floods, droughts, and storms that killed the crops and left the families and their livestock with very little food. Quilt blocks tell the story of western weather, good and bad.

THE·WEATHER QUILT BLOCKS

Enduring all kinds of weather, pioneer women recorded
wind and sun in the patterns of their quilt blocks.

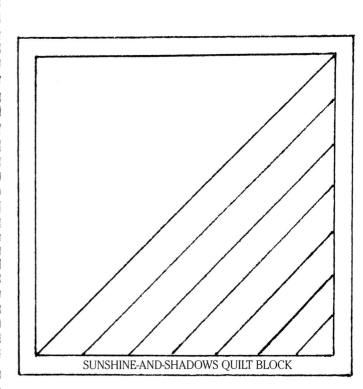

SUNSHINE-AND-SHADOWS QUILT BLOCK

My Weather Diary

To make a weather diary you will need copies of the diary cover and the insert page. Cut out both on heavy lines; fold on dotted lines. Staple to form booklet. Record the weather for one week. Keep the diary in a safe place for a year. Then look in your diary and compare the past weather with the weather now. Many pioneers kept diaries. By reading those diaries we can learn what it was like to be a pioneer.

WEATHER ☇ DIARY

WEATHER DIARY INSERT PAGE

1.	5.
2.	6.
3.	7.
4.	*Your name:* _____

FOLLOWING A STAR

It took less than a hundred years for the pioneer families of America to settle the land west of the eastern seaboard. In the process the United States was formed. When I look at a map of our country, I like to think it resembles a gigantic patchwork quilt sewed together by the brave pioneers.

Some people say the pioneers hitched their wagons to a star and followed their dreams. Do you think that this might be the reason that star shapes were the most frequently used patterns in quilt blocks?

Quilts made by the pioneer women were valued possessions and were passed down in families to succeeding generations. We call those quilts heirlooms. Often heirloom quilts are displayed in museums. Many other heirloom quilts are kept in private collections.

When you view a quilt, study the patterns and shapes in the quilt blocks. See if you can find a special story in the quilt's design.

SPECIAL STAR QUILT BLOCKS

Star quilt blocks were named for places, events, and people in the lives of the pioneers. Here are four very special stars.

STAR OF THE WEST

OHIO STAR

MARTHA WASHINGTON'S STAR

LEMOYNE OR LEMON STAR

HANGING WINDMILL STAR

To make a hanging windmill star you will need scissors, medium-weight paper, markers or crayons, glue, several strips of tissue paper 1 inch (2.5 centimeters) wide and 12 inches (30 centimeters) long, a paper punch, and string.

Make two copies of the windmill star quilt block. Color them, and glue them together back-to-back. Punch a hole at the black dot. Attach string for hanging. Attach several tissue streamers at the opposite corner, and hang the star to turn in the breeze.

FOR FURTHER READING

ABOUT PIONEER DAYS:

Emsden, Katharine. *Voices From the West: Life Along the Trail.* Discovery Enterprises, 1993.

Fisher, Leonard Everett. *The Oregon Trail.* New York: Holiday House, 1990.

Knight, Amelia Stewart. *The Way West: Journal of a Pioneer Woman.* New York: Simon & Schuster, 1993.

McCall, Edith. *Wagons Over the Mountains.* Chicago: Childrens Press, 1980.

Smith, Carter, ed. *Bridging the Continent; A Sourcebook on the American West.* Brookfield, Connecticut: The Millbrook Press, 1992.

ABOUT QUILTS:

Coerr, Eleanor. *The Josefina Story Quilt.* New York: HarperCollins, 1986.

Lyons, Mary E. *Stitching Stars: The Story Quilts of Harriet Powers.* New York: Scribners, 1993.

Paul, Ann W. *Eight Hands Round: A Patchwork Alphabet.* New York: HarperCollins, 1991.

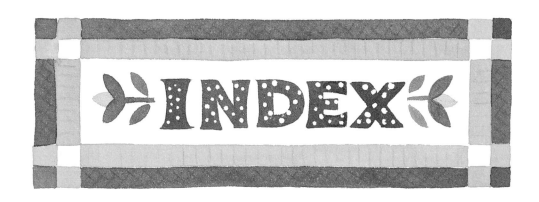

INDEX